Iron Horses Across America:
The Transcontinental Railroad

edited by Jeanne Munn Bracken

Major Trans-Mississippi and Pacific Railroads

LINE	COMPLETED	LINE	COMPLETED
1. Union Pacific	1869	7. Northern Pacific	1883
2. Central Pacific	1869	8. Denver/Rio Grande	1883
3. Kansas Pacific	1870	9. Texas & Pacific	1882
4. Denver Pacific	1871	10. Southern Pacific	1883
5. Oregon Short Line	1882	11. Santa Fe	1883
6. Oregon Ry.& Nav.	1884	12. Great Northern	1893

© Discovery Enterprises, Ltd.
Carlisle, Massachusetts

© Discovery Enterprises, Ltd., Carlisle, MA 1995
ISBN 1-878668-36-6 paperback edition
Library of Congress Catalog Card Number 95-68773

10 9 8 7 6 5 4 3 2 1

Printed in the United States of America

Subject Reference Guide

Cataloging in Publication Data:

Iron Horses Across America: The Transcontinental Railroad
edited by Jeanne Munn Bracken
Railroads — United States — History
Central Pacific Railroad Company
Union Pacific Railroad Company

Dewey: 385.09   LC: HE 2763

Photo & Illustration Credits

(p. 11) Edwin Tunis; (p. 20) "Across the Continent," by Fanny Palmer
(Currier and Ives); (p. 23) Union Pacific Railroad; (p. 29) by Paul Frenzeny for
Harpers; (p. 33) California Historical Society; (p. 38) Library of Congress;
(p. 45) Pinkerton's Inc.; (p. 55) Chicago Historical Society.

Acknowledgments

The following books provided original source materials as noted:

Annals of America, vol. 7 & 8

A Treasury of Railroad Folklore, edited by B.A. Botkin and Alvin F. Harlow

Makin' Tracks, edited by Lynn Rhodes Mayer and Kenneth E. Vose

The editor is also grateful as always for the assistance and support of her
colleagues at the Lincoln (MA) Public Library and throughout the Minuteman
Library System, especially at the Acton Memorial Library and Beverly Shank
(Medford Public Library), and for the refuge provided by the Reuben Hoar
Library in Littleton for over two decades. Jeanne Rondoe and other friends
with the SCBWI also deserve recognition as hand-holders *extraordinaire.*

Table of Contents

Dedication

Dedicated to the memory of Grandpa Munn and my father-in-law Donald Bracken, who helped make the trains run.

Grandpa was a railroad man,
Erie Lackawanna;
I married the son of a railroad man,
Denver and Rio Grande. . .

Railroad in American History

by
Jeanne Munn Bracken

Early transportation in America depended to a great degree on waterways: rivers, coastal shipping, canals. Slowly, rough roads were built from the centers of population into the countryside, but they weren't very effective for moving goods and people from one place to another, especially over long distances.

Enter the railroads. The earliest rail cars were simple coaches or wagons set on tracks and pulled by horses. Cars with sails blown by the wind were an interesting experiment but didn't prove very useful. A side or head wind would push the car in the wrong direction or just over onto its side. Horses on treadmills in the middle of passenger cars were another experiment; although they reached the respectable speed of twelve miles per hour, they didn't catch on either.

The invention of the steam locomotive in England in 1814 was therefore a great leap forward in the history of transportation. Still, steam locomotives fueled by wood had their own difficulties. Early passenger cars were open coaches set on tracks. Sparks rained on the riders, with predictable results: travelers had to put out fires in their clothing. Depending on the direction of the prevailing winds, one side of the tracks was smokier and more fire-prone than the other. This smokier side was less desirable, growing into the poorer side of town. Hence, the phrase "the wrong side of the tracks". The flying ember problem didn't really clear up until coal became the fuel of choice.

Railroads were not invented in America, to be sure. Rather, the English had expanded on the idea of horsedrawn trams. The English built passenger railroads between cities: Liverpool and Manchester, London and Birmingham.

5

Americans picked up on the notion, using short railroad lines built for specific purposes like hauling lumber, stone, or other goods to waterways for long distance transport via ship. The first working railroad in America (1826) was the short line built to carry blocks from the granite quarries of Quincy, Massachusetts, to barges on the Neponset River. Ferried across Boston Harbor, the stone was used to build the Bunker Hill Monument. The rail line ran all of three miles.

Other early railroads were also short stretches of track connecting the Pennsylvania coal mines with the canals, or carrying lumber to the rivers for floating downstream to sawmills, or hauling ore from the gold mines. Drawn by horses or relying on gravity, they provided a tiny cog in a vast continent's transportation system.

In 1830 there were only twenty-three miles of railroad track in the country, but by 1840 most states east of the Mississippi River had some track, 590 miles in all, still mostly in short lines. Gauges (the distance between the rails on the track) varied between four and six feet. The standard gauge, 4'8 1/2," was finally set in 1862 by Abraham Lincoln, allowing rolling stock (cars and locomotives) for the first time to be usable from one company's track to another.

The English invented railroads and made them work between civilized points. It took the Americans to build railroads, at enormous effort and expense, that at first went virtually nowhere, through nearly uncharted, unpopulated, and hostile climates and Indian territory.

The English built railroads for the present day. It took the Americans to build them into the future.

The "Iron Horse"

(From *Walden,* by Henry David Thoreau)

Henry David Thoreau, born in Concord, Massachusetts in 1817, was a poet, essayist, and philosopher. His best-known work, *Walden, or Life in the Woods*, was published in 1854, several years after he left his cabin at Walden Pond.

... As I sit at my window this summer afternoon, hawks are circling about my clearing...and for the last half-hour I have heard the rattle of railroad cars, now dying away and then reviving like the beat of a partridge, conveying travellers from Boston to the country. ...

The Fitchburg Railroad touches the pond about a hundred rods south of where I dwell. I usually go to the village along its causeway, and am, as it were, related to society by this link. The men on the freight trains, who go over the whole length of the road, bow to me as to an old acquaintance, they pass me so often, and apparently they take me for an employee; and so I am. I too would fain be a track-repairer somewhere in the orbit of the earth.

The whistle of the locomotive penetrates my woods summer and winter, sounding like the scream of a hawk sailing over some farmer's yard, informing me that many restless city merchants are arriving within the circle of the town, or adventurous country traders from the other side. ... Here come your groceries, country; your rations, countrymen! ... Up comes the cotton, down goes the woven cloth; up comes the silk, down goes the woollen; up come the books, but down goes the wit that writes them. ... when I hear the iron horse make the hills echo with his snort like thunder, shaking the earth with his feet, and breathing fire and smoke from his nostrils ..., it seems as if the earth had got a race now worthy to inhabit it.

What's the railroad to me?
I never go to see
Where it ends.
It fills the hollows,
And makes banks for the swallows.
It sets the sand a-blowing,
And the blackberries a-growing,

but I cross it like a cart-path in the woods. I will not
have my eyes put out and my ears spoiled by its smoke
and steam and hissing. (Henry David Thoreau, *Walden,*
New York: Dodd, Mead & Company, 1946, pp. 119-129)

The whistle of the Fitchburg to Boston locomotives, diesel
now, still sing across the water's surface on summer afternoons.

Rails Across the Continent

by
Jeanne Munn Bracken

The earliest American railroads were short lines built for
specific freight hauling. They were followed by lines between
population centers from the East Coast to the Mississippi River.
Especially with the gold rush of the 1840s, the far westward
movement pushed beyond the heartland. Miners and settlers were
generally headed for the West Coast. Along the way there were
few to greet them except a handful of soldiers at lonely forts and
a lot of unfriendly Native Americans.

These settlers and fortune seekers had a choice of travel
options, none of them particularly efficient or inexpensive. They
could spend four to eight months with a wagon train from the
Mississippi River to Oregon or other coastal points. They could
take a ship from an eastern port around the tip of South America
and up the Pacific to California; this 15,000 mile journey consumed six to eight months. They could take a ship part way,

8

crossing the disease-ridden Isthmus of Panama; the trip took about a month and cost $300, for those willing to risk the short-cut. As trails were established in the 1850s, stagecoaches made the bumpy run from the midwest to California; this was fairly fast but very expensive. Or they could walk, as many Mormons did, pushing their goods in wheelbarrows.

Some, of course, were perfectly happy with the status quo. The stagecoach companies, innkeepers along the route, overland freighters, steamship lines, canalmen and riverboatmen didn't want the competition of railroads that threatened their livelihood. (The riverboatmen were also concerned that railroad bridges would create obstacles for their ships.) The Indians, had they been represented in Congress, surely would have been opposed to what amounted to a grab for some of their land.

Realists knew, too, of the difficulties that building such a railroad would entail. The terrain varied from desert to steep mountains. There were virtually no services available along the route.

Men had been thinking of a railroad across the American continent for years, but as the 1860s dawned, the nation was mired in the Civil War. The war was to some extent both good news and bad news for the dreamers. The Civil War showed once and for all how important railroads were for moving soldiers and supplies quickly from one hot spot to another. The North, with its miles of track and manufacturing centers for locomotives and other railroad equipment, had a distinct advantage over the more agricultural South. On the other hand, the four-year war consumed manpower, financial resources, and the attention of the policymakers in Washington.

Still, those who favored building a railroad across the land were not content to stand quietly by. One of those was Theodore Judah, an easterner transplanted to California. Earlier proponents were dreamers and schemers without practical expertise or even interest in the awesome feat that building a railroad across empty plains and towering mountains would require. Judah, on the other hand, had railroad experience and the drive to finally get the project underway.

He needed, of course, financing. Eventually Judah formed a partnership with four Californians: dry goods merchant Charles Crocker, wholesale grocer Leland Stanford, and hardware store owners Collis P. Huntington and Mark Hopkins (The Big Four). It didn't hurt at all that Stanford became the Governor of California before the project was well underway. None of the men was wealthy (yet), so Judah went to Washington to seek funding.

Civil War era investors were making plenty of money peddling munitions and other military supplies. They were not especially interested in long-shot investments like a railroad. So Congressional generosity was necessary—and was given. The results were the Railway Acts of 1862 and 1864 that authorized government bonds and land grants for the companies building a transcontinental railroad. The Union Pacific, for example, was granted nearly 10% of the land area of Nebraska alone.

The big railroad backers (the Big Four of the Central Pacific and Thomas Durant of the Union Pacific) realized that there was a lot of money to be made in just building the railroads. It didn't matter where the tracks were going or if they ever carried a single shipment of passengers and freight. Their fortunes were made.

The Central Pacific was built without Theodore Judah. The engineer wanted to spend the time and money to build a proper railroad and do it right. His partners wanted to build it fast and cheap. When Judah was forced out, he headed back for Washington to seek different backers. On the trip across the Isthmus of Panama, he contracted a fatal illness and died shortly after reaching New York.

The Central Pacific owners stretched an investment of $150,000 into $200,000,000 in profits just in the building, not counting the seventeen and a half million acres of real estate that enriched them through their wheeling and dealing. Greed, cheating, and fraud were the games they played. The developers of the

Union Pacific were no better. Both railroad companies bribed federal, state and local officials, blackmailed towns along the proposed route, and lined their own pockets by forming separate companies to do the actual construction. The resulting scandals colored the country's history for decades.

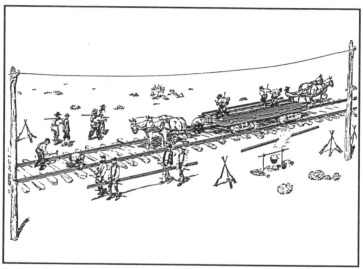

Laying the track, by Edwin Tunis

The Central Pacific broke ground in Sacramento on January 8, 1863, to the amusement of bystanders. The Union Pacific broke ground on December 8, 1863, and never laid another foot of track for a full year. They started for real when Grenville Dodge came on board after the Civil War ended.

All the expected difficulties arose—and more. Indians attacked surveying crews, which often worked well ahead of the track builders; they also tore up survey stakes and caused accidents by blocking the tracks. The huge buffalo herds that thundered across the plains were another problem; they damaged track and knocked down telegraph poles, which they discovered made fine scratching posts during molting season.

Weather was another enemy of the railroad construction crews. Bitter snowy winters halted most construction in the Sierra Nevadas. Spring thaws in the mountains and on the plains turned streams and dry gulches into raging torrents that washed out track and trestles. Thunderstorms, wind, drought, avalanche, dust storms — all these tormented the railroads. And still they built.

The Central Pacific didn't have much trouble with the Native Americans; they allowed them to ride free whenever they wanted. By the spring of 1869, they had laid 690 miles of track over, around, and through the Sierra Nevadas into Utah. The Union Pacific, building over easier terrain, covered 1095 miles of plains, foothills, and Rocky Mountain passes into Utah.

The two lines met at Promontory Summit, Utah, on May 10, 1869. The continent was conquered.

Your Memorialist, Asa Whitney

One of the earliest to propose a transcontinental railroad was Asa Whitney, a New Yorker who made a fortune in the China trade. In 1845, he proposed to Congress that he be granted a strip of land sixty miles wide from the Great Lakes to the Pacific in order to build a railroad. Whitney was not so much interested in opening up the continent, which he believed to be more or less worthless in large part, as in promoting the railroad as a shorter route to the Pacific, the better to transship goods to and from the Orient. On January 28, 1845, Whitney petitioned Congress:

> Your memorialist begs respectfully to represent to your honorable body that, by rivers, railroads, and canals, all the states east and north of the Potomac connect directly with the waters of the Great Lakes.

That there is a chain of railroads in projection and being built from New York to the southern shore of Lake Michigan, which, crossing all the veins of communication to the ocean through all the states south and east of the Ohio river, will produce commercial, political, and national results and benefits which must be seen and felt through all our vast Confederacy. Your memorialist would further represent to your honorable body that he has devoted much time and attention to the subject of a railroad from Lake Michigan, through the Rocky Mountains, to the Pacific Ocean; and that he finds such a route practicable, the results from which would be incalculable, far beyond the imagination of man to estimate. To the interior of our vast and widely spread country it would be as the heart is to the human body.

It would, when completed, cross all the mighty rivers and streams which wend their way to the ocean through our vast and rich valleys, from Oregon to Maine, a distance of more than 3,000 miles. ...It would enable us in the short space of eight days (and perhaps less) to concentrate all the forces of our vast country at any point, from Maine to Oregon, in the interior or on the coast.

Such easy and rapid communication, with such facilities for exchanging the different products of the different parts, would bring all our immensely widespread population together as one vast city, the moral and social effects of which must harmonize all together as one family with but one interest—the general good of all.

...Then the drills and sheetings of Connecticut, Rhode Island, and Massachusetts can be transported to China in thirty days, and the teas and rich silks of China in exchange come back to New Orleans, to Charleston, to Washington, to Baltimore, to Philadelphia, to New York, and to Boston in thirty days more.

...Your memorialist begs respectfully to represent further, to your honorable body, that he can see no way or means by which this great and important work can be accomplished, for ages to come, except by a grant of a sufficient quantity of the public domain...

...Your memorialist would respectfuly represent, further, to your honorable body that, from an estimate as nearly accurate as can be made short of an actual survey, the cost of said road, to be built in a safe, good and substantial manner, will be about $50 million; and as the road cannot (from the situation of the uninhabited country through which it will pass) earn anything or but little before its completion, therefore a further sum of $15 million will be required to keep in operations, expenses, etc.—making the total estimated cost of said road, when completed, $65 million.

It may require some years before the earnings of said road...can be much if anything beyond its current expenses for repairs, etc...It would be the only channel for the commerce of all the western coast of Mexico and South America, of the Sandwich Islands (Hawaii), of Japan, of all China, Manila, Australia, Java, Singapore, Calcutta, and Bombay—not only all ours but the commerce of all Europe.

To the most of these places must pass this road—your memorialist says *must* because the saving of time (so all-important to the merchant) from the long and hazardous voyage around either of the capes would force it; and in a few years would be built up cities, towns and villages, from the lake to the ocean, which would alone support the road.

...Your memorialist respectfully represents, further, to your honorable body, that, from the knowledge he can procure, he finds that the lands, for a long distance east of the mountains, are bad, of litttle or no value for culture; that through and for some distance beyond the mountains would also be of but little if any value; therefore, your memorialist is satisfied that it will require an entire tract of sixty miles in width, from as near Lake Michigan as the unappropriated lands commence to the Pacific Ocean.

...your memorialist is induced to pray that your honorable body will grant to himself, his heirs and assigns such tract of land, the proceeds of which to be strictly and faithfully applied to the building and completing the said road, always with such checks and guarantees to your honorable body as shall secure a faithful performace of all the obligations and duties of your memorialist;...

Your memorialist further prays that your honorable body will order a survey of said route, to commence at some point to be fixed upon as most desirable on the shore of Lake Michigan, between the 42o and 45o north latitude, thence west to the gap or pass in the mountains, and thence the most practicable route to the Pacific Ocean.

Whitney was ahead of his time. He was asking for an enormous portion of the unclaimed lands of the plains and mountains. Congress was not yet ready to make such a concession, any more than they were ready to choose a route. Whitney may have been a visionary or just a shrewd businessman, but he was wrong about one thing. The transcontinental railroad never became a major player in the Europe to China trade route—because the Suez Canal opened in 1869, the same year the Central Pacific and Union Pacific met at Promontory Summit, Utah. Goods moving between Europe and the Orient were spared the long and dangerous passage around the Cape of Good Hope at the tip of Africa.

Setting the Route: A Political Venture

Many obstacles stood in the way of building the railroad.
First, there was all that emptiness in the middle of the continent.
While visionaries could see benefits in opening the territory,
many practical thinkers saw only a huge expense with little
return. Among those who were convinced of the value of the
railroad, many were interested mainly in their own profit. They
wanted the road to start in their own backyard and travel to the
west coast, and they were willing to vote against any proposal
that took a different route. Politics, too, played an important
role in the 1850s. Southern slave states didn't want the railroad
to go north of them, cutting them out of the loop, and northern-
ers didn't want to benefit the south by running the tracks west
from their lands. It wasn't until 1862, when the southern states
had seceded from the union, that the first Railway Act was finally
passed. That legislation approved government grants for the
building of the railroad, grants of both land and bonds to make
the transcontinental a reality. Abraham Lincoln set the eastern
terminus in Omaha, where he happened to own some land. The
western end would be in Sacramento. Nobody thought to set the
site at which the two, the Union Pacific building westward and
the Central Pacific building eastward, would meet. That failing
led to some of the most colorful exploits of the whole enter-
prise. Nor, despite surveys in the 1850s, was any exact route
set. Parties of surveyors moved ahead of the track builders, finding the best way across the plains and through the mountains.
The railroad builders threatened and blackmailed those few who
were already on the plains or in the mountains; if they didn't
pay, the railroad bypassed them and the resulting economic boom
went elsewhere.

"A railroad company approaches a small town as a highwayman approaches his victim. The threat, 'If you do not accede to our terms we will leave your town two or three miles to the side!' is as efficacious as the 'Stand and deliver,' when backed by a cocked pistol. For the threat of the railroad company is not merely to deprive the town of the benefits which the railroad might give; it is to put it in a far worse position than if no railroad had been built...And just as robbers unite to plunder in concert and divide the spoil, so do the trunk lines of railroads unite to raise rates and pool their earnings, or the Pacific roads form a combination with the Pacific Mail Steamship Company by which toll gates are virtually established on land and ocean." (Henry George, "Progress and Poverty," 1879, pp. 192-193. Quoted in *The Robber Barons,* by Matthew Josephson, New York: Harcourt Brace and Co., 1934)

The Railroad Builds a Town

Frithjof Meidell wrote to his family in Norway in 1855:

Dear Mother:

I received Hansine's letter a couple of days ago, and I was indeed glad to hear that all of you are getting along so well. The same is true of Christian and me; both of us are feeling fine. I have tried many a ruse to get him to write home, but all in vain. A real porker, that fellow! ...I...see that you now have both railroad and telegraph. Hurrah for old Norway!

How is the railroad getting along? Here in America it is the railroads that build up the whole country. Because of them the farmers get wider markets and higher prices for their products. They seem to put new life into everything. Even the old apple woman sets off at a dogtrot when she hears that whistle to sell her apples to the passengers. Every ten miles along the railways there are stations, which soon grow up into town. "Soon," did I say? I should have said "immediately," because it is really remarkable how rapidly the stations are transformed into little towns. I can but compare it with the building of Aladdin's castle by means of his wonderful lamp, only that things move still faster here, where it is not necessary to sit and rub a rusty old oil lantern. Here you can buy houses all ready to be placed on the freight car, and in half a day's time they can be nailed together.

Since I have nothing else to write about this time, I shall attempt to describe how these towns spring up. First—that is, after the two old log houses that stand one on each side of the tracks—first, I say, the railroad company builds a depot. Next, a speculator buys the surrounding 100 acres and lays it out in lots, streets, and a marketplace. Then he graces the prospective town with the name of an early President or a famous general—or his own name—holds an auction, and realizes many hundred percent on his investment.

A young wagonmaker who has just completed his apprenticeship hears about the station, that it is beautifully located in a rich farming country, is blessed with good water, and, most important of all, that it has no wagonmaker. Making a hasty decision, he buys the barest necessities for setting up in his profession, hurries off to the place, rents one of the old log houses, and is soon at work. One absolute necessity he still lacks, however: a sign, of course, which is the most important part of a man's equipment here in America. The next day he hears that there is a tramp painter aboard the train; he gets him off, puts him to work, and the very next day the farmers are surprised to see a monstrous sign straddling the roof of the old log house.

The sign is an immediate success, for the farmers rush to the shop and order wagons, wheels, and the like. The

18

poor man is overwhelmed with more work than he can handle for ever so long. He is about to regret that sign notion of his, but suddenly he has another idea. He accepts every order, and no sooner are the customers away than he seizes his pen and writes to the editors of three different newspapers that three good apprentices can secure steady work with high wages in the "flourishing town of L." Within two days he has help enough, and the work goes "like a song."

The train stops again, and off steps a blacksmith who went broke in one of the larger towns. He saunters over to the wagonmaker's shop as unconcerned as if he only wished to light his cigar. In a casual way he inquires about the neighborhood and wonders what its prospects are, without indicating that he intends to settle there—by no means! But the wagoner, with his keen Yankee nose, soon smells a rat and starts boosting the place with all his might. This inspires the smith with ecstasy; he starts jumping around and making sledgehammer motions with his arms. Off he goes and rents the other log house and nails a horseshoe over the door as a sign. The horseshoe, to be sure, cannot be seen at any great distance, but the smith has a remedy for this, and he starts to hammer and pound away at his anvil so that the farmers for miles around can hear the echoes. They immediately flock to his door, and there is work enough for the blacksmith.

Within a short week, a carpenter, a tailor, and a shoemaker also arrive in town. The wagoner orders a house from the carpenter and rents the second story to the tailor and the shoemaker. Soon the blacksmith also builds a house, and things progress with giant strides toward the bigger and better.

Again the train stops. This time two young fellows jump off, look around, and go over to have a chat with the blacksmith. One of them is a doctor, the other a lawyer. Both of them rent rooms from the blacksmith and start business.

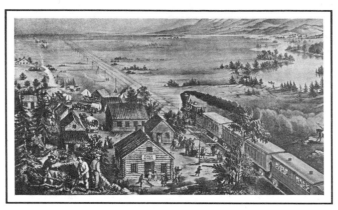

Towns sprung up overnight along the railroad.

Once more the locomotive stops. But—what's this getting off? Be patient! Just let it come closer. It is nothing more nor less than a mustacioed, velvet-frocked German with an old, overworked hurdy-gurdy strapped to his back. On the hurdy-gurdy perches a measly little monkey dressed in red. The German goes over to the blacksmith shop and begins to crank his music box while the monkey smokes tobacco, dances a polka, and grinds coffee. But the German receives no encouragement for his art, nor does the monkey—except some rusty nails which the smith tosses to him. The artist realizes that his audience is very unappreciative, and the poor man's face is overcast with sorrow.

Then he looks about inquiringly as if searching for something and steps up to the doctor to ask if there is a restaurant in town. On receiving a negative reply, his face brightens again; and after a short conversation with the doctor and lawyer, he steams off with the next train and jumps off at the first big town, where he sells his hurdy-gurdy and monkey and buys a barrel of whiskey, another barrel of biscuits, two large cheeses, tobacco, cigars, and sausages—miles of them. Thereupon he engages a painter to make an appropriate sign, and in three days he is back again in the new town. Now he rents the blacksmith's old log house and rigs it up as a shop. Soon the sign swings over the door, the whiskey barrel is half empty, and the sausages are dispatched by the yard.

...His best customers are the railroad workers, most of whom are Irishmen. ...I believe I must have mentioned them before. They consist mostly of the worst riffraff of Europe, to whom America is a promised land where you earn a dollar a day and are not hanged for stealing. When these roughnecks get together it is a pretty dull party unless there are a couple of fights and someone gets a good hiding. As you go along a railway under construction, it is easy to detect the places where they have had their frolics by the torn-up sod, the tufts of hair, the broken bottles, pipes, pants' buttons, blood, and so forth, which they have left behind them.

...But to get back to my town again. The German, the blacksmith, and the tailor do a rushing business. The train stops again, and this time it is a printer who makes his appearance. He gets in touch with the doctor and lawyer; an old printing press is for sale in the next town; they buy it, and with this new event we can really say that the town has "arrived." Some little trouble there is, to be sure, concerning the political affiliations of the paper, because it develops that the lawyer is a Democrat, the doctor an Abolitionist, and the printer a Whig. But a compromise is soon reached and the paper announces itself as "independent." The lawyer volunteers to write the editorials, while the doctor promises a wealth of death announcements, and the German and the blacksmith undertake to fill the rest of the paper with advertisements.

Within a few years the town is very large. The wagonmaker owns practically half of it. The German deals only in wholesale. The lawyer is mayor of the town, and the blacksmith does nothing but smoke cigars, for now he is a man of affluence. (*Archives of America*, vol. 8, pp. 349-353)

Meidell's attitude towards the Irish was by no means unusual. So unpopular were they that the sign "No Irish need apply" was common in the New World. Yet during the Civil War, when labor was scarce and the railroads needed men, the Irish found their niche and made a mighty contribution to the expansion of their new nation.

While Meidell wrote with a bit of exaggeration about the growth of cities and towns along the railroad routes, there is surely more than a kernal of truth to his letter. On the other hand, those towns bypassed by the railroads (often because they refused to be blackmailed) saw a decline in their fortunes. Witness the following story:

Why Danville Lost a Railroad

Dressed as a plain surveyor, bespattered with muddy water, a stranger registered in the old Gilcher House, Danville, Ky., and was assigned to an attic bedroom with a dormer window, a shuck-mattress bed, and a tallow-dip candle, in the late (18)60's. The unknown guest demanded a decent room for the night. This infuriated the clerk, who sized up the stranger and exclaimed: "That room is plenty good for the looks of you!"

Thereupon the infuriated "surveyor" wrote across the page of the hotel register:

"Surveyors: locate the road just far enough away from Danville so its citizens can barely hear the whistles blow. (Signed) E. D. Standiford, President of the Louisville and Nashville R. R. Co."

Sequel to the above: To this day, sixty odd years later, Danville passengers must hire taxis and drive three miles to catch an L&N train for east or west. To assuage their grief, awakened citizens of Danville induced the Cincinnati Southern Railway to survey its municipally owned 'Queen and Crescent' route via Danville... (By Col. C.E. Woods, youngest L&N station agent to 1884, Sidney, Illinois, in *Time*, reprinted in *Railroad STories*, vol. XV, October 1934, No. 3, p. 64. Copyright, 1934, by the Frank A. Munsey Company, New York. From: *A Treasury of Railroad Folklore,* B. A. Botkin and Alvin F. Harlow, eds. New York: Crown Publishers, Inc., 1953)

Workers on the Union Pacific lower heavy stones to build an abutment over the Green River.

Building the Railroads:
The Irish and the Chinese

Both the era and the isolation of the terrain were responsible for an important shortage in building the first transcontinental railroad. In many areas, for both the Union Pacific building west and the Central Pacific moving east, there wasn't enough wood, water, or other necessities. But finding workers was the major difficulty for both companies.

Part of the problem was the timing. The railroads began to build during the Civil War, when much of the country was engaged in fighting each other. When the war ended in 1865, freed prisoners, defeated southerners, and former soldiers went to work on the railroads. But in the meantime, two groups of immigrants who might not have found work in easier times were recruited to hew the lines through the mountains and across the prairies.

In the midwest, the Union Pacific took on tough, brawling, hard-drinking Irishmen, who were not welcome at more genteel jobs. On the West Coast, the Central Pacific turned to an unlikely source of labor, the Chinese.

Many were skeptical that the frail, tiny Chinese could perform the heavy work required to hack away mountainsides, leveling areas for tracks, or that they would have the stamina to withstand the extremes of climate. Still, in promoting the use of the Asians, one official noted that the Chinese had built the Great Wall and should be useful to the railroads. After watching them for a brief period, their detractors were won over. Charles Crocker, a principal of the Central Pacific and one of the Big Four, testified later how and why the Chinese were given a chance.

The Celestials

"I recollect that I had a great deal of trouble to get Mr.
Strobridge (the construction leader) to try Chinamen. At
first I recollect that four or five of the Irishmen on pay day
got to talking together and I said to Mr. Strobridge there
is some little trouble ahead. When I saw this trouble im-
pending, a committee came to us to ask for an increase of
wages. I told Mr. Strobridge then to go over to Auburn
and get some Chinamen and put them to work. The result
was the Irishmen begged us not to have any Chinamen
come, and they resumed their work. It was four or five
months after that before I could get Mr. Strobridge to take
Chinamen. Finally he took in fifty Chinamen, and a
while after that he took in fifty more. Then, they did so
well that he took fifty more, and he got more and more
until finally we got all we could use, until at one time I
think we had ten or twelve thousand." (From *Makin'
Tracks: The Story of the Transcontinental Railroad in the
pictures and words of the men who where there*, edited by
Lynn Rhodes Mayer and Kenneth E. Vose. New York:
Praeger Publishers, Inc., 1975, p. 28)

E. B. Crocker, Charles' brother, wrote a letter in 1865 regard-
ing the Chinese:

"...A large part of our force are Chinese and they prove
nearly equal to white men in the amount of labor they
perform, and are far more reliable. No danger of strikes
among them. We are training them to all kinds of labor,
blasting, driving horses, handling rock, as well as the pick
and shovel." (Ibid, p. 28)

25

The Chinese were paid the same as the whites, except that their board was not included. A report to the government by Leland Stanford, another of the Big Four and by then governor of California, noted in the fall of 1865:

"The greater portion of the laborers employed by us are Chinese who constitute a large element in the population of California. Without them it would be impossible to complete the western portion of this great national enter-prise within the time required by the Acts of Congress.

As a class they are quiet, peaceable, patient, industrious and economical—ready and apt to learn all the different kinds of work required in railroad building, they soon become as efficient as white laborers. More prudent and economical, they are contented with less wages. We find them organized into societies for mutual aid and assis-tance. These societies, that count their numbers by thou-sands, are conducted by shrewd, intelligent businessmen, who promptly advise their subordinates where employ-ment can be found on the most favorable terms.

...Their wages, which are always paid in coin at the end of each month, are divided among them by their agents, who attend to their business, in proportion to the labor done by each person. These agents are generally American or Chinese merchants, who furnish them their supplies of food, the value of which they deduct from their monthly pay." (From *Makin' Tracks: The Story of the Transcontinental Railroad in the pictures and words of the men who where there*, edited by Lynn Rhodes Mayer and Kenneth E. Vose. New York: Praeger Publishers, Inc., 1975, p. 31)

While the Caucasian workers were subsisting on a diet of beef, potatoes, bread and butter, the Chinese were enjoying a variety of foods including dried fishes, dried bamboo shoots, mushrooms, dried seaweed, pork, poultry, rice, fruit, peanut oil, Chinese bacon, and more. The tea that the Chinese preferred had an additional benefit: boiling the water spared them some of the illnesses that struck the others.

Winter brought bitter cold to the Chinese and the others digging through the Sierra Nevada Mountains. Avalanches killed workmen. Winds and deep snow slowed or stopped trains. The same snows that had stopped the ill-fated Donner wagon party not so many years before, at the same gap in the peaks that was named for them, Donner Pass, stopped the railroad builders as well. More than a few froze to death along the tracks and trails.

Yet before they were finished, the Central Pacific crews would build thirteen tunnels through the Sierras, the longest 1695 feet in length—hacked through granite and shale.

Chinese immigrants arriving in San Francisco to help build the Central Pacific Railroad.

The Terrestrials

The Central Pacific had solved its labor shortage with
the Chinese (Celestials). The Union Pacific, meanwhile, had
ex-soldiers and a new army of Irish railroad workers. These
refugees from the Potato Famine were not welcome in most
manufacturing jobs of the northeast. They were good workers,
but their rowdy leisure activities created all sorts of problems.
They were known as Terrestrials, for they were surely earthy.
All of their needs, from food to fuel, had to be hauled to their
camps by special trains that came to be known as Hell on
Wheels.

The Union Pacific got off to a slow start. Practically everything was in short supply. Yet, once they got going under super-
organizers Jack and Dan Casement, they made up for lost time.
Horse-drawn rail cars carried rails to the worksite, where they
were quickly unloaded and the cars returned to the supply site
to pick up more. Spikes and ties were dropped along the track,
exactly where they would be needed. Each man had a specific job,
and even when it was finished for the day, he didn't get far from
the tracks.

Working through lands peopled mostly by hostile natives
with a few soldiers for protection, the crews saw towns grow
overnight at the end of the tracks. There they could spend their
money on liquor, women and gambling. "Hell on Wheels,"
though, supplied their basic needs.

> The front of Casement's train is a truck laden with
> such sundries as switch stands, targets, ...timbers for
> truck repairs, iron rods, steel bars, barrels, boxes...
> straight-edges, wrenches...cable, rope, cotton waste...
> mattresses... with a blacksmith shop in full blast in
> rear.

In the second car is the feed store and saddler's shop. The third is the carpenter shop and wash-house...The fourth is a sleeping apartment for mule-whackers. Fifth, a general sleeping car with bunks for 144 men. Sixth, sitting and dining room for employees. Seventh, long dining room at the tables of which 200 men can be comfortably seated. Eighth, kitchen in front and counting room and telegraph office in rear. Ninth, store car. Tenth through sixteenth, all sleeping cars. Seventeenth and eighteenth, Captain Clayton's cars: the former his kitchen; the latter his parlor...Nineteenth, sleeping car. Twentieth, supply car. Twenty-first and twenty-second, water cars. (From *Deseret News*, Salt Lake City, April 23, 1869, as quoted in *Makin' Tracks: The Story of the Transcontinental Railroad in the pictures and words of the men who where there*, edited by Lynn Rhodes Mayer and Kenneth E. Vose. New York: Praeger Publishers, Inc., 1975, p. 72)

The dining cars had a single long table down the middle with the tin plates nailed in place. When workers were finished eating their hasty meals, they often just climbed onto the table to get over and escape. The sleeping cars had bunks in three tiers as well as hammocks hanging under them and even tents on the roof. Refinements were rare, and rarer still with the graders, who worked on separate teams some distance ahead of even the questionable civilization of "Hell on Wheels", preparing the landscape for the tracks.

There are no managers or secretaries connected with a grading outfit; there are bosses and timekeepers. One of the first tents to go up is the hotel tent, and the man who runs it is the boarding boss. He is usually a jolly, fearless man, a good hustler, but not necessarily addicted to real manual toil. His wife does that. From four in the morning until midnight, this slave of the camp is on her feet. To be sure, there are men cooks and flunkies and dishwashers, but the boarding boss has but one wife, and she must oversee everything. She must see that nothing goes to the pigs until all the boarders have refused it. Her tired but ever-smiling face repels more kicks than a State militia could repel. If one of the drivers is kicked by a mule, she bathes his hurt with horse liniment, and allows the wounded man to sit in the rocking-chair in the eating tent...She is at once a mother to the beardless and sister of charity to the bearded men. Her private tent is the one spot respected at all times by the rough men of the camp, whether they be drunk or sober. (Cy Warman in *Makin' Tracks: The Story of the Transcontinental Railroad in the pictures and words of the men who where there*, edited by Lynn Rhodes Mayer and Kenneth E. Vose. New York: Praeger Publishers, Inc., 1975, p. 78)

The Irish working on the railroads were also known as tarriers. Their job in later years was to stand beside the steam drills and move the loose rock. This well-known folksong was written by a tarrier named Thomas Casey.

Drill, Ye Tarriers, Drill

Ev'ry morning at seven o'clock
There was twenty tarriers a-working at the rock,
And the boss comes along, and he says kape still,
And come down heavy on the cast iron drill,
And drill, ye tarriers, drill!

Chorus
Drill, ye tarriers, drill!
It's work all day for sugar in your tay;
Down behind of the railway,
And drill, ye tarriers, drill,
And blast! and fire!

The boss was a fine man down to the ground,
And he married a lady six feet round.
She baked good bread and she baked it well,
But she baked it hard as the holes in hell,
And drill, ye tarriers, drill!

The new foreman was Jean McCann,
By God, he was a blame mean man.
Last week a premature blast went off,
And a mile in the air went big Jim Goff,
And drill, ye tarriers, drill!

When the next pay day came round,
Jim Goff a dollar short was found.
When he asked, "What for?" came this reply,
"You're docked for the time you was up in the sky."
And drill, ye tarriers, drill!

(From *Fireside Book of Folk Songs*, by Margaret
Bradford Boni. New York: Simon and Schuster, 1947,
pp. 138-9)

Promontory Point

No point had been fixed for the Central Pacific and the Union Pacific tracks to meet. Originally the Central Pacific was supposed to cross the Sierra Nevada Mountains and stop, but the Railroad Act of 1864 allowed them to keep going. Since they received government grant money for each mile of road they completed, each company was eager to get as large a portion as possible. The final months of construction became a contest to see which railroad could get the farthest in the fastest time. This competition culminated in a legendary day, April 29, 1869, when the Central Pacific crews laid ten miles and fifty-six feet of track in one twelve-hour day. As the end neared, the companies sabotaged each other's work.

It took a Joint Resolution of Congress to set the final meeting point at Promontory Summit, Utah—fifty-six miles west of Ogden and bypassing Brigham Young's Mormon community at Salt Lake City to the south.

A ceremony marking the union was held at Promontory on May 10, 1869, two days behind schedule. The trainload of Central Pacific dignitaries had been delayed by an accident in the Sierras and the Union Pacific bigwigs by a washout at the Devil's Gate Bridge in Wyoming. The joining was symbolized by the driving of four special spikes (only one of them gold).

One was inscribed "May God continue the unity of our country as this Railroad unites the two great Oceans of the world." Lofty expectations indeed for rival companies who had been warring only days before! Leland Stanford of the Central Pacific and Thomas Durant of the Union Pacific each took a mighty swing to drive the ceremonial spike. Both missed, to the amusement of the construction crews standing by.

The Rev. Todd of Massachusetts invoking a blessing on the joining of Union and Pacific railroads.

The race had captured the imagination of Americans on both coasts much as the space race did a century later—but without modern communication methods. Those were the days of newspapers and, at the end, it was the newfangled telegraph, whose lines marched across prairie and mountain pass with the tracks, that carried the message: Done! The continent was bound by iron rails.

Bret Harte (1836 - 1902) was born in New York State and went to California on the heels of the miners. His short stories about life in the towns made him famous, but he was also a poet. In later years he served as a diplomat in Prussia and Scotland; he lived the end of his life in London. Harte was popular for a time but lost favor with editors and readers as the quality of his work slipped. His earliest stories, like "The Luck of the Roaring Camp" and "The Outcasts of Poker Flat" are best remembered today.

What the Engines Said

by Bret Hart

(The joining of the Union Pacific and Central Pacific Railroads)

May 10, 1869

What was it the Engines said,
Pilots touching,—head to head
Facing on the single track,
Half a world behind each back?
This is what the Engines said,
Unreported and unread.

With a prefatory screech,
In a florid Western speech,
Said the engine from the WEST:
"I am from Sierra's crest;
And if altitude's a test,
Why, I reckon, it's confessed
That I've done my level best."

Said the Engine from the EAST:
"They who work best talk the least.
S'pose you whistle down your brakes;
What you've done is no great shakes.-
Pretty fair,—but let our meeting
Be a different kind of greeting.
Let these folks with champagne stuffing,
Not their Engines, do the puffing.

"Listen! Where Atlantic beats
Shores of snow and summer heats;
Where the Indian autumn skies
Paint the woods with wampum dyes,—
I have chased the flying sun,
Seeing all he looked upon,
Blessing all that he has blessed,
Nursing in my iron breast

All his vivifying heat,
All his clouds about my crest;
And before my flying feet
Every shadow must retreat."

Said the Western Engine, "Phew!"
And a long, low whistle blew.
"Come, now, really, that's the oddest
Talk for one so very modest.
You brag of your East! You do?
Why, I bring the East to you!
All the Orient, all Cathay,
Find through me the shortest way;
And the sun you follow here
Rises in my hemisphere.
Really,—if one must be rude,—
Length, my friend, ain't longitude."

Said the Union: "Don't reflect, or
I'll run over some Director."
Said the Central: "I'm Pacific;
But, when riled, I'm quite terrific.
Yet to-day we shall not quarrel,
Just to show these folks this moral,
How two Engines—in their vision—
Once have met without collision."

This is what the Engines said,
Unreported and unread;
Spoken slightly through the nose,
With a whistle at the close.

Immigrants and Outlaws

Even before the final spike was driven into the Utah soil, the railroads were seeking immigrants for several reasons. First, the settlers would pay the transit fares to their new lands. Second, they would buy land from the railroad, acreage that had been given to the companies by the government as construction incentive. Third, they would purchase freight and goods shipped to them from other areas of the country. Fourth, they would pay to ship their crops to other cities and towns—via the railroad. The companies not only monopolized cross-continental shipment, they controlled the choicest waterfront properties and warehouse locations, extending their influence far beyond the sound of the train's whistle. The companies mounted massive advertising campaigns that stretched or buried the hard truth.

Scandinavians, Germans, Russians, Welshmen, Scots—all were lured to the American interior by agents who targeted the poorest of European peasants. Here, they were promised, was the true "Land of Milk and Honey." No mention was made of blizzards, dust storms, insect plagues, periodic droughts, prairie fires, and the multitude of other challenges the settlers would face.

The agents outdid themselves with wild assurances. There might not be, they acknowledged, enough wood for fuel, but the settlers could always dig for coal—in Kansas! The fertile soil would yield twenty-pound radishes, four-pound potatoes, massive crops of wheat per acre.

Those worried about vast arid stretches of wilderness were assured that it had been scientifically proven: plowing the land would draw more rain, and locomotives and the railroads themselves would cause more rain to fall. Changing the climate of the great plains was just a masterful stroke of the pen for these corporate liars.

European governments saw an opportunity here. While they were often reluctant to see their citizens leaving their homelands, they also saw a golden opportunity to send some of their less productive folks somewhere else. So paupers and convicts had their passage paid to the New World.

Like the Chinese and Irish before them, these Europeans proved to be made of sturdy stock. Place names all across North America bear reminders even today of those early settlers who may not have found coal in Kansas, but who came and stayed anyway.

Robert Louis Stevenson (1850-1894) was born in Scotland, died in Samoa, and lived for a time in the United States. Although Across the Plains *wasn't published until 1892, it was written some fifteen years earlier, relating the poet/novelist's experiences riding the immigrant train from the Missouri to San Francisco. After completion of the first section of the transcontinental railroad in 1869, the ride across the country was faster than by wagon train or stagecoach, but it was not necessarily more comfortable. Those who could afford it rode in relative style; a second group of passengers (mostly those traveling from one inland city to another rather than the entire cross-country trip) had some comforts, but those usually poorer folks relocating from the east to the west coast's Promised Land used special cars. These were sparsely furnished, as Stevenson describes, and were often shuttled aside for faster trains to pass. While they were not the fastest trains, they were the cheapest. Stevenson, on his way to the Pacific, was not planning to settle in America, as were many of his fellow travelers.*

On the Immigrant Train

...It was about two in the afternoon of Friday that I found myself in front of the Emigrant House (near Council Bluffs, Iowa), with more than a hundred others, to be sorted and boxed for the journey. A white-haired official, with a stick under one arm, and a list in the other hand, stood apart in front of us, and called name after name in the tone of a command. At each name you would see a family gather up its brats and bundles and run for the hindmost of the three cars that stood awaiting us, and I soon concluded that this was to be set apart for the women and children. The second or central car, it turned out, was devoted to men travelling alone, and the third to the Chinese.

Inside a rail car, called "The Modern Ship of the Plains."

...I suppose the reader has some notion of an American railroad-car, that long, narrow wooden box, like a flat-roofed Noah's ark, with a stove and a convenience (toilet), one at either end, a passage down the middle, and transverse benches upon either hand. Those destined for emigrants on the Union Pacific are only remarkable for their extreme plainness, nothing but wood entering in any part into their constitution, and for the usual inefficacy of the lamps, which often went out and shed but a dying glimmer even while they burned. The benches are too short for anything but a young child. Where there is scarce elbow-room for two to sit, there will not be space enough for one to lie. ...Hence the company... prevail upon every two to chum together. To each of the chums they sell a board and three square cushions stuffed with straw, and covered with thin cotton. The benches can be made to face each other in pairs, for the backs are reversible. On the approach of night the boards are laid from bench to bench, making a couch wide enough for two, and long enough for a man of the middle height; and the chums lie down side by side upon the cushions with the head to the conductor's van and the feet to the engine. When the train is full, of course this plan is impossible, for there must not be more than one to every bench...

...A great personage on an American train is the newsboy. He sells books (such books!), papers, fruit, lollipops, and cigars; and on emigrant journeys, soap, towels, tin washing dishes, tin coffee pitchers, coffee, tea, sugar, and tinned eatables, mostly hash or beans and bacon...

There were meals to be had, however, by the wayside: a breakfast in the morning, a dinner somewhere between eleven and two, and supper from five to eight or nine at night. We rarely had less than twenty minutes for each; and if we had not spent many another twenty minutes waiting for some express upon a side track among miles of desert, we might have taken an hour to each repast and arrived at San Francisco up to time. For haste is not the foible of an emigrant train. It gets through on sufferance, running the gauntlet among its more considerable bretheren; should there be a block, it is unhesitatingly sacrificed; and they cannot, in consequence, predict the length of the passage within a day or so. Civility is the main comfort that you miss. Equality, though conceived very largely in America, does not extend so low down as to an emigrant. Thus in all other trains, a warning cry of "All aboard!" recalls the passengers to take their seats; but as soon as I was alone with emigrants, and from the Transfer all the way to San Francisco, I found this ceremony was pretermitted; the train stole from the station without note of warning, and you had to keep an eye upon it even while you ate. The annoyance is considerable, and the disrespect both wanton and petty.

Many conductors, again, will hold no communication with an emigrant. I asked a conductor one day at what time the train would stop for dinner; as he made no answer I repeated the question, with a like result; a third time I returned to the charge, and then Jack-in-office looked me coolly in the face for several seconds and turned ostentatiously away. I believe he was half ashamed of his brutality; for when another person made the same inquiry, although he still refused the information, he condescended to answer, and even to justify his reticence in a voice loud enough for me to hear. It was, he said, his principle not to tell people where they were to dine; for one question led to many other questions, as what o'clock it was? or, how soon should we be there? and he could not afford to be eternally worried.

...It had thundered on the Friday night, but the sun rose on Saturday without a cloud. We were at sea—there is no other adequate expression—on the plains of Nebraska. ...It was a world almost without a feature; an empty sky, an empty earth; front and back, the line of railway stretched from horizon to horizon, like a cue across a billiard-board; on either hand, the green plain ran till it touched the skirts of heaven. Along the track innumerable wild sunflowers, no bigger than a crown-piece, bloomed in a continuous flower-bed; grazing beasts were seen upon the prairie at all degrees of distance and diminution; and, now and again we might perceive a few dots beside the railroad which grew more and more distinct as we drew nearer till they turned

40

into wooden cabins, and then dwindled and dwindled in our wake until they melted into their surroundings, and we were once more alone upon the billiard-board...

At Ogden we changed cars from the Union Pacific to the Central Pacific line of railroad. The change was doubly welcome; for, first, we had better cars on the new line; and, second, those in which we had been cooped for more than ninety hours had begun to stink abominably. ...But one thing I must say, the car of the Chinese was notably the least offensive.

The cars on the Central Pacific were nearly twice as high, and so proportionally airier; they were freshly varnished, which gave us all a sense of cleanliness as though we had bathed; the seats drew out and joined in the centre, so that there was no more need for bedboards; and there was an upper tier of berths which could be closed by day and opened at night.

...Of all stupid ill-feelings, the sentiment of my fellow-Caucasians towards our companions in the Chinese car was the most stupid and the worst. They seemed never to have looked at them, listened to them, or thought of them, but hated them a priori. ...They could work better and cheaper in half a hundred industries, and hence there was no calumny too idle for the Caucasians to repeat, and even to believe. ...my emigrants declared that the Chinese were dirty. I cannot say they were clean, for that was impossible upon the journey; but in their efforts after cleanliness they put the rest of us to shame. We all pigged and stewed in one infamy, wet our hands and faces for half a minute daily on the platform, and were unashamed. But the Chinese never lost an opportunity, and you would see them washing their feet—an act not dreamed of among ourselves—and going as far as decency permitted to wash their whole bodies...

...The Chinese are considered stupid, because they are imperfectly acquainted with English. They are held to be base, because their dexterity and frugality enable them to

underbid the lazy, luxurious Caucasian. ...Awhile ago it
was the Irish, now it is the Chinese that must go. Such
is the cry... (Excerpted from *The Travels and Essays of
Robert Louis Stevenson*, by Robert Louis Stevenson.
New York: Charles Scribner's Sons, 1895, pp. 115-140)

The discomforts of the train were nothing compared to the
disasters and perils many of the immigrants faced as they settled
the heartland of the American continent. Many nonetheless pre-
vailed. Enclaves of Scandinavians and Germans, Russians and
Mennonites in the midwest bear witness even today to their
determination.

---

*For the earliest travelers on the transcontinental railroad,
the hazards included hastily built bridges and spindly trestles
spanning rivers and deep canyons. These were weakened by the
weather (snow, spring thaws, and floods) and sometimes deliber-
ately by hostile Indians eager to rid their lands of the white in-
truders. Rail beds laid on poorly prepared ground had to be re-
built. And then came the outlaws. The transcontinental railroad
was barely finished before some realized how easy it would be
to rob trains passing through the desolate center of the continent.
Some of our most enduring legends of the West involved train
robbers: Butch Cassidy, the Sundance Kid, and the James brothers. Writer O. Henry turned his comic, skewed attention to this
phenomenon in one of his short stories.*

Holding up a Train

NOTE The man who told me these things was for
several years an outlaw in the Southwest and a follower of
the pursuit he so frankly describes. His description of the
modus operandi should prove interesting, his counsel of

value to the potential passenger in some future "hold up," while his estimate of the pleasures of train robbing will hardly induce any one to adopt it as a profession. I give the story in almost exactly his own words. O. H.

Most people would say, if their opinion was asked for, that holding up a train would be a hard job. Well, it isn't; it's easy. I have contributed some to the uneasiness of railroads and the insomnia of express companies, and the most trouble I ever had about a hold-up was in being swindled by unscrupulous people while spending the money I got. The danger wasn't anything to speak of, and we didn't mind the trouble.

One man has come pretty near robbing a train by himself; two have succeeded a few times; three can do it if they are hustlers, but five is about the right number. The time to do it and the place depend upon several things.

The first "stick-up" I was ever in happened in 1890. ...Being mighty hard up, we decided to transact a little business with the railroads. Jim and I joined forces with Tom and Ike Moore—two brothers ... I can call their names, for both of them are dead. Tom was shot while robbing a bank in Arkansas; Ike was killed during the more dangerous pastime of attending a dance in the Creek Nation.

We selected a place on the Santa Fe where there was a bridge across a deep creek surrounded by heavy timber. All passenger trains took water at the tank close to one end of the bridge. It was a quiet place, the nearest house being five miles away. The day before it happened, we rested our horses and "made medicine" as to how we should get about it. Our plans were not at all elaborate, as none of us had ever engaged in a hold-up before.

The Santa Fe flyer was due at the tank at 11:15 p.m. At eleven, Tom and I lay down on one side of the track, and Jim and Ike took the other. As the train rolled up, the headlight flashing far down the track and the steam hissing from the engine, I turned weak all over. I would have worked a whole year on the ranch for nothing to have been out of that affair right then. Some of the nerviest men in the business have told me that they felt the same way the first time.

The engine had hardly stopped when I jumped on the running-board on one side, while Jim mounted the other. As soon as the engineer and fireman saw our guns they threw up their hands without being told, and begged us not to shoot, saying they would do anything we wanted them to.

"Hit the ground," I ordered, and they both jumped off. We drove them before us down the side of the train. While this was happening, Tom and Ike had been blazing away, one on each side of the train, yelling like Apaches, so as to keep the passeners herded in the cars. Some fellow stuck a little twenty-two calibre out one of the coach windows and fired it straight up in the air. I let drive and smashed the glass just over his head. That settled everything like resistance from that direction.

I made the fireman get a lantern, and then I went to the express car and yelled to the messenger to open up or get perforated. He slid the door open and stood in it with his hands up. "Jump overboard, son," I said, and he hit the dirt like a lump of lead. There were two safes in the car —a big one and a little one. By the way, I first located the messenger's arsenal—a double-barrelled shot-gun with buckshot cartridges and a thirty-eight in a drawer. I drew the cartridges from the shot-gun, pocketed the pistol, and called the messenger inside. I shoved my gun against his nose and put him to work. He couldn't open the big one, but he did the little one. There was only nine hundred dollars in it. That was mighty small winnings for our trouble, so we decided to go through the passengers. We took our prisoners to the smoking-car, and from there sent the engineer through the train to light up the coaches...

PROCLAMATION

OF THE

GOVERNOR OF MISSOURI!

REWARDS

FOR THE ARREST OF

Express and Train Robbers.

STATE OF MISSOURI,
EXECUTIVE DEPARTMENT.

WHEREAS, It has been made known to me, as the Governor of the State of Missouri, that certain parties, whose names are to me unknown, have confederated and banded themselves together for the purpose of committing robberies and other depredations within this State; and

WHEREAS, Said parties did, on or about the Eighth day of October, 1879, stop a train near Glendale, in the county of Jackson, in said State, and, with force and violence, take, steal and carry away the money and other express matter being carried thereon; and

WHEREAS, On the fifteenth day of July 1881, said parties and their confederates did stop a train upon the line of the Chicago, Rock Island and Pacific Railroad, near Winston, in the County of Daviess, in said State, and, with force and violence, take, steal, and carry away the money and other express matter being carried thereon; and, in perpetration of the robbery last aforesaid, the parties engaged therein did kill and murder one WILLIAM WESTFALL, the conductor of the train, together with one JOHN McCULLOCH, who was at the time in the employ of said company, then on said train; and

WHEREAS, FRANK JAMES and JESSE W. JAMES stand indicted in the Circuit Court of said Daviess County, for the murder of JOHN W. SHEETS, and the parties engaged in the robberies and murders aforesaid have fled from justice and have absconded and secreted themselves:

NOW, THEREFORE, in consideration of the premises, and in lieu of all other rewards heretofore offered for the arrest or conviction of the parties aforesaid, or either of them, by any person or corporation, I, THOMAS T. CRITTENDEN, Governor of the State of Missouri, do hereby offer a reward of five thousand dollars ($5,000.00) for the arrest and conviction of each person participating in either of the robberies or murders aforesaid, excepting the said FRANK JAMES and JESSE W. JAMES; and for the arrest and delivery of said

FRANK JAMES and JESSE W. JAMES,

and each or either of them, to the sheriff of said Daviess County, I hereby offer a reward of five thousand dollars, ($5,000.00,) and for the conviction of either of the parties last aforesaid of participation in either of the murders or robberies above mentioned, I hereby offer a further reward of five thousand dollars, ($5,000.00.)

IN TESTIMONY WHEREOF, I have hereunto set my hand and caused to be affixed the Great Seal of the State of Missouri. Done

[SEAL.] at the City of Jefferson on this 28th day of July, A. D. 1881.

THOS. T. CRITTENDEN.

By the Governor:

MICH'L K. McGRATH, Sec'y of State.

...There were very few people in the day coaches at that time of night, so we made a slim haul until we got to the sleeper. The Pullman conductor met me at one door while Jim was going round to the other one. He very politely informed me that I could not go into that car, as it did not belong to the railroad company, and, besides, the passengers had already been greatly disturbed by the shouting and firing. Never in all my life have I met with a finer instance of official dignity and reliance upon the power of Mr. Pullman's great name. I jabbed my six-shooter so hard against Mr. Conductor's front that I afterward found one of his vest buttons so firmly wedged in the end of the barrel that I had to shoot it out. He just shut up like a weak-springed knife and rolled down the car steps.

I opened the door of the sleeper and stepped inside. A big, fat, old man came wabbling up to me, puffing and blowing. He had one coat-sleeve on and was trying to put his vest on over that. I don't know who he thought I was.

"Young man, young man," says he, "you must keep cool and not get excited. Above everything, keep cool."

"I can't," says I. "Excitement's just eating me up." And then I let out a yell and turned loose my forty-five through the skylight.

The old man tried to dive into one of the lower berths, but a screech came out of it, and a bare foot that took him in the bread-basket and landed him on the floor. I saw Jim coming in the other door, and I hollered for everybody to climb out and line up.

They commenced to scramble down, and for a while we had a three-ringed circus. The men looked as frightened and tame as a lot of rabbits in a deep snow. They had on, on an average, about a quarter of a suit of clothes and one shoe apiece. One chap was sitting on the floor of the aisle, looking as if he were working a hard sum in arithmetic. He was trying, very solemn, to pull a lady's number two shoe on a number nine foot.

The ladies didn't stop to dress. They were so curious to see a real, live train robber, bless 'em, that they just wrapped blankets and sheets around themselves and came out, squeaky and fidgety looking. They always show more curiosity and sand than the men do.

We got them all lined up and pretty quiet, and I went through the bunch. I found very little on them—I mean in the way of valuables. One man in the line was a sight. He was one of those big, overgrown, solemn snoozers that sit on the platform at lectures and look wise. Before crawling out he had managed to put on his long, frock-tailed coat and his high silk hat. The rest of him was nothing but pajamas and bunions. When I dug into the Prince Albert, I expected to drag out at least a block of gold mine stock or an armful of Government bonds, but all I found was a little boy's French harp about four inches long. What it was there for, I don't know. I felt a little mad because he had fooled me so. I stuck the harp up against his mouth.

"If you can't pay—play," I says.

"I can't play," says he.

"Then learn right off quick," says I, letting him smell the end of my gun-barrel.

He caught hold of the harp, turned red as a beet, and commenced to blow. He blew a dinky little tune...

I made him keep on playing it all the time we were in the car. Now and then he'd get weak and off the key, and I'd turn my gun on him and ask what was the matter, ...which would make him start up again like sixty. I think that old boy standing there in his silk hat and bare feet, playing his little French harp, was the funniest sight I ever saw. One little red-headed woman in the line broke out laughing at him. You could have heard her in the next car.

47

Then Jim held them steady while I searched the berths. I grapped around in those beds and filled a pillow-case with the strangest assortment of stuff you ever saw. Now and then I'd come across a little pop-gun pistol, just about right for plugging teeth with, which I'd throw out the window. When I finished with the collection I dumped the pillow-case load in the middle of the aisle. There were a good many watches, bracelets, rings and pocket-books, with a sprinkling of false teeth, whiskey flasks, face-powder boxes, chocolate caramels, and heads of hair of various colors and lengths. There were also about a dozen ladies' stockings into which jewelry, watches, and rolls of bills had been stuffed and then wadded up tight and stuck under the mattresses. I offered to return what I called the "scalps," saying that we were not Indians on the warpath, but none of the ladies seemed to know to whom the hair belonged.

One of the women—and a good-looker she was— wrapped in a striped blanket saw me pick up one of the stocking that was pretty chunky and heavy about the toe and she snapped out:

"That's mine, sir. You're not in the business of robbing women, are you?"

Now, as this was our first hold-up, we hadn't agreed upon any code of ethics, so I hardly knew what to answer. But, anyway, I replied: "Well, not as a specialty. If this contains your personal property you can have it back."

"It just does," she declared eagerly, and reached out her hand for it.

"You'll excuse my taking a look at the contents," I said, holding the stocking up by the toe. Out dumped a big gent's gold watch, worth two hundred, a gent's leather pocket-book, that we afterward found to contain six hundred dollars, a 32-calibre revolver and the only thing of the lot that could have been a lady's personal property was a silver bracelet worth about fifty cents.

I said, "Madame, here's your property," and handed her the bracelet. "Now," I went on, "how can you expect us to act square with you when you try to deceive us in this manner? I'm surprised at such conduct."

The young woman flushed up as if she had been caught doing something dishonest. Some other woman down the line called out: "The mean thing!" I never knew whether she meant the other lady or me.

When we finished our job we ordered everybody back to bed, told 'em good-night very politely at the door, and left. We rode forty miles before daylight and then divided the stuff. Each one of us got $1752.85 in money. We lumped the jewelry around. Then we scattered, each man for himself.

That was my first train robbery, and it was about as easily done as any of the ones that followed. But that was the last and only time I ever went through the passengers. I don't like that part of the business. Afterward I stuck strictly to the express car. ...

I don't think I ought to close without giving some deductions from my experience of eight years "on the dodge." It doesn't pay to rob trains. Leaving out the question of right and morals, which I don't think I ought to tackle, there is very little envy in the life of an outlaw. After a while money ceases to have any value in his eyes. He gets to looking upon the railroads and express companies as his bankers, and his six-shooters as a cheque book good for any amount. He throws away money right and left. Most of the time he is on the jump, riding day and night, and he lives so hard between times that he doesn't enjoy the taste of high life when he gets it. He knows that his time is bound to come to lose his life or liberty, and that the accuracy of his aim, the speed of his horse, and the fidelity of his "sider," are all that postpone the inevitable. (From *The Complete Works of O. Henry*, by O. Henry. New York: Doubleday and Company, 1953. pp. 831-839)

The Legend of John Henry

The completion of the transcontinental railroad was only the beginning of the race to reach every part of the continent by rail. From central points in the east, west, south and north, tracks reached like fingers grasping for new towns and cities. Fortunes were still to be made—and lives to be lost. One of the most famous legends of any railroad age was John Henry, a steel-driving man (one who hammered the spikes into the rails). The Big Bend Tunnel in West Virginia was part of the Chesapeake and Ohio Railroad, built around 1870. He was probably based on a real African American, but his story has become a myth, larger than life. Many versions of this song have been passed down from generation to generation for over a century. John Henry did beat the steam drill, but he burst a blood vessel and died trying.

John Henry

When John Henry was a little baby
Sittin' on his mammy's knee
Says, "The Big Bend Tunnel on the C&O Road,
Gonna be the death of me, Lawd, Lawd,
Gonna be the death of me."

John Henry had a little woman
And she was always dressed in blue,
She went down track never looking back,
Says, "John Henry, I am always true to you,
    Lawd, Lawd!
John Henry, I am always true to you."

John Henry had a pretty little boy,
Sittin' in the palm of his hand.
He hugged and kissed him an' bid him farewell,
"Oh son, do the best you can, Lawd, Lawd!
Son, do the best you can."

John Henry said to his captain,
"A man ain't nothing but a man.
An' before I'll let your steam drill beat me down,
Die with the hammer in my hand, Lawd, Lawd,
Die with the hammer in my hand."

John Henry got a thirty pound hammer,
Beside the steam drill he did stand.
He beat that steam drill three inches down,
An' died with his hammer in his hand, Lawd, Lawd,
Died with his hammer in his hand.

They took John Henry to the graveyard
An' buried him in the sand,
An' ev'ry locomotive come roarin' by
Says, "Dere lays a steel-drivin' man, Lawd, Lawd!
Dere lays a steel-drivin' man."

So every Monday mornin'
When the bluebirds begin to sing,
You can hear those hammers a mile or more,
You can hear John Henry's hammer ring, Lawd, Lawd,
You can hear John Henry's hammer ring.

There are many versions of the John Henry legend. These verses are taken from *The Fireside Book of Folk Songs*; the final verse is adapted from *A Natural Man, The True Story of John Henry*.

Laying the Rails and
Lining Their Pockets

Even before the first rails were laid, the financial razzle-dazzle began. The builders were determined to line their own pockets. To keep the competition to a minimum, both the Union Pacific and the Central Pacific formed subsidiaries to do the actual construction, essentially hiring themselves—at a handsome profit. In one especially daring move, the Central Pacific moved the Sierra Nevada Mountains twenty-four miles to the west—at least on paper. Since the railroads would receive $16,000 in government bonds for each mile built on the plains, $32,000 for each mile in the foothills, and $48,000 for each mountain mile, it was to their advantage to have as much of the route designated mountainous as possible. Using a land survey that showed Sierra-type soil a short distance from San Francisco, the Central Pacific management told the government in faraway Washington that the mountains started at that point. President Lincoln approved the plan and the railroad was paid at the mountain rate to build across the nearly flat coastal plain. This "move" netted the Central Pacific an additional $768,000.

The speed with which the railroads were racing across the continent, the competition to build the longer road for its financial benefits, the distance from the Washington government, the isolation of the construction—all were factors that gave the railroads something of a free rein. The railroad barons used it to the fullest. Some government officials and Congressmen, too, had been given stock in the railroads to enlist their support. Still, Washington was aware that all was not as it should be with the railroads. In January 1869, months before the golden spike was hammered into Utah soil at Promontory, Ulysses S. Grant appointed C. H. Snow as a government director of the Union

Pacific. The President sent the new official west to check things out. Snow's report found much to criticize. (It is interesting to note that the investigation and report took less than two months to complete—without the use of computers, telephones, airplanes, or FAX machines.)

Report on Building the Union Pacific

While this report evaluates the Union Pacific, their rivals at the Central Pacific shared most, if not all, of the practices. Excerpts from C. H. Snow's report follow.

Washington, D.C. March 5th, 1869

To the President:

Having on the 9th day of January 1869, been appointed a Government Director of the Union Pacific Railroad, I deemed it necessary, and was requested by the President at the earliest practicable day, to make myself acquainted with the condition and management of that road.

I therefore proceeded to Omaha, and instituted a careful personal examination, which I prosecuted not only to the end of the line as far as cars are running, but several miles beyond.

I now have the honor to submit a partial and preliminary report, as to the location, construction, and condition of the road, as I found it.

Under the act creating this company, they are required, before they can receive any of the subsidies granted, to complete so many consecutive miles of a road, supplied with all necessary drains, culverts, viaducts, crossings, sidings, bridges, turnouts, watering places, depots, equipments, furniture, and all other appurtenances of a first class railroad.

(Snow continues with a bit of history, noting that in 1866 the Secretary of the Interior had directed that both the Union Pacific and the Central Pacific conform to construction standards and set up boards to determine those standards. The members of those boards, Snow notes, "were evidently (and perhaps properly) animated by a feeling of liberality toward the Union Pacific..." The Union Pacific took full advantage of that friendliness.)

...Two important reports have recently been made in respect to the condition of the U.P.R.R. ...It appears by both of these reports, not only that the Company have not constructed a "first class railroad," but they have in many things utterly disregarded the specifications proscribed by the board herein before mentioned.

...One case will furnish as example. (An earlier report) stated that Dale Creek, on the western slope of the Black Hills, running in a granite gorge 120 feet deep and two feet wide at grade line, was crossed by a pine timber trestle bridge of 40 feet spans; and complained that it was exposed to decay, and especially to fire. The remedy applied has been to lay a floor upon the bridge, and paint it with fireproof paint. (The report) suggested that, "when the bridges shall decay, permanence should be given, either by filling the gorge with earth and rock, or by an iron bridge resting on stone piers."

It strikes me that waiting for the bridge to decay would be rather hazardous. Its decay might, and perhaps will, be discovered by its giving way under a train. But it is so fixed now that the unsuspecting passengers will not see their danger, nor know that the yawning chasm, granite bottomed, into which they are plunging is one hundred and twenty feet deep!

The gist of the (second report) is contained in that part of it which contains an estimate of what it will cost to make the first 890 miles of the road west of Omaha such a road as was contemplated by the Act of Congress. The amount necessary to do this they estimate at Six million, four hundred and eighty-nine thousand, five hundred and fifty dollars. And this, it must be remembered, is for completing a portion of the road which had been accepted as *completed*, and paid for by the government!

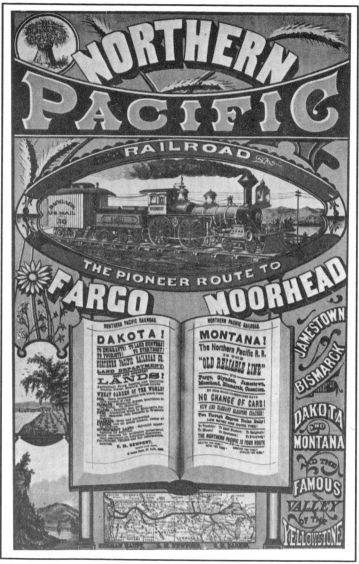

The Northern Pacific Railroad, like other lines, promoted the travel to the Western territories by rail.

...There are drains where there ought to be culverts, and fillings where there ought to be drains. For one thousand miles west of Omaha, there are two arched culverts, and only two! On the 13th of February, between Shell Creek and North Bend, the track and embankment for about 400 feet were washed away, for want of sufficient drainage. A freight train drawn by Engine No 126 (which had been but two months on the road) ran into the chasm, completely wrecking the engine and several cars. A passenger train might have met the same fate.

...In regard to these subjects [water tanks and windmills], I can now only very briefly make a partial report. The Watertanks are at convenient distances, and are nearly all provided with wind mills, furnished by the "Maynard Wind Mill Company," with which to pump water.

If the company had any way of regulating the wind, these things would be both economical and useful. As it is, however, whatever may be said in favor of their economy, they certainly do not possess utility. When there is no wind they do not work; and when there is any wind in that country, there is too much for these mills; their machinery is thrown out of gear and they will not pump.

In a few instances stationary engines have been substituted for the wind mills; and at Bryan there are 36 men employed at $3.00 per day each to work the wind mill. Yet these mills are still being erected, a circumstance accounted for by some bad people, who assert that the "Maynard Windmill Company" is composed of the managers of the road.

...The track is laid under a contract with Casement Bro's, in which, it is said, at least two persons connected with the management of the road have an interest.

The price paid is $800 per mile when not over two miles per day are laid; if over two miles the price is $1,200. When detentions occur, by reason of the roadbed not being ready, the contractors receive $3,000 per day for such detentions.

(Snow's report continues, complaining that for the last one hundred miles accepted, joints had been laid in what was at best a temporary manner.)

Such a track may do for a short time, but I have no knowledge of any other road, "first class" or otherwise, that has adopted this plan of laying a track.

It has but one advantage—and that one may answer all the purposes of the managers of the road—which is that more track can be laid in a day than if the joints were required to be placed on ties.

As to (ballasting), I have only time to say there is little or none on the road.

I approach the subject of management of this road with great reluctance—partly because of its delicacy, and partly because of its magnitude. But as the subject cannot be treated of with delicacy and at the same time with truth, I must eschew the former for the sake of the latter. The fact is, the road is not managed at all. It is mismanaged altogether.

It might be supposed that the managers of this company, in selecting a person to superintend such a road—the longest line of road in the world—would have cast about them for a man of experience—a man who had not only been a railroad man, but a successful superintendent of railroads. The position is one of unparalelled difficulties in the history of railroading.

The experience of the General Superintendent as a railroad man, before entering upon the duties of General Superintendent of this, the greatest of roads, was all gained by selling tickets for a railroad in the interior of Iowa.

Is any further explanation necessary as to why this road is so fearfully mismanaged? Only this, that he openly proclaims, and acts upon the theory, that there shall be no man employed upon the road, who knows more about railroading than he does! Commencing with superlative inefficiency, and adopting a descending scale, is surely not the best way to successfully manage a great line of railroad...

The road is divided into four divisions, each of which is under the charge of a division Superintendent—one of whom I will state, at the risk of causing his dismissal, does know more about railroading than the General Superintendent. These Division Superintendents operate their respective divisions as though each was a seperate (sic) road, and each competing with each other. Instead of harmony in their operation there is jealousy; instead of cooperation there is antagonism. They are not willing to assist each other—neither will they ask nor accept the assistance of the others, lest the General Superintendent should say (as he would) that he would have no division Superintendent who could not take care of his own division under any and all circumstances.

Better, they reason, that everything should go wrong or stand still than that the general Superintendent should come to regard them as so far lacking in ability and energy as to require assistance; and from their stand-point they reason well. The same feeling porvades (sic) all the employees of the road. Each is anxious to stand well with the general superintendent; and each is afraid that the other will outdo him in gaining the favor of this great man.

Jealousy among equals, and tyranny on the part of superiors, are universal.

One incident, which occurred at Rawlings Springs on the 13th of February, illustrates the chances of an employee, who has a mind of his own, holding his place.

An engineer was directed to take out an engine—which he declined to do, stating it would burst. He was dismissed. Another engineer was ordered to take out the engine, but gave the same answer and shared the same fate. A third engineer received the same order, and obeyed it. Within half an hour the engine exploded, killing the engineer, fireman and conductor.

The effects of the mismanagement of the road are seen and felt everywhere—in the rusty locomotives in the engine houses, in the dead locomotives (including about one-half of those owned by the Company), in the trains abandoned and forgotten, in the vexatious delays of freight shipped over the road. (There are instances where freight has been delayed on the road for two months or more; and in some cases it never was heard of after leaving Omaha.) The public who furnish the means to build the road, are certainly entitled to better management of it than they now have.

Snow's report contains sections on finances showing that the railroad companies were paying a lot more to build than it had cost earlier companies in other areas of the country; their balance sheets showed them in debt. They did not take into account, however, the value of the lands given to the companies by the government. The acreage might not have been worth very much at the time it was given, but it certainly increased in value as the trains rolled by. And of course, the company was overpaying itself to do the construction.

It is a fact which no one doubts, and I believe no one denies, that the persons who have had the superintendance and management of the construction of the Union Pacific Railroad are the persons who have been, and are, the contractors for its construction.

The "credit mobilier" does the work and receives the money. And what is the "credit mobilier?" To use the forcible language of Charles Frances Adams, Jr., in an article in the *North American Review* for January 1869, "It is but another name for the Pacific Railroad Ring. The members of it are in Congress; they are trustees for the bond-holders, they are directors, they are stockholders, they are contractors; in Washington they vote the studies, in New York they receive them, upon the Plains, they expend them, and in the 'credit mobilier' they divide them.

"Ever shifting characters, they are ever ubiquitous, they receive money into one hand as a corporation, and pay it into the other as a contractor. ...

"As stockholders they own the road, as mortgagees they have a lien upon it, as directors they contract for its construction, and as members of the 'credit mobilier' they build it."

It will be thus seen that these parties are not only deeply interested in getting all the money they can, but also in spending all they get; which circumstance will account for the immense cost of constructing the road, as reported by the company.

In this connection I will say that I encountered difficulties almost insurmountable in attempting to gain information in regard to the details of the management of the road. ...In the few instances where I gained information from employees, they had a fear and openly expressed it, that they would loose (sic) their places if I used their names in connection with the information they gave.

No one, however, can pass over the line, and observe what is going on, without feeling that all and more than all that has ever been charged against the management of the road is true....

To build a railroad faster than even Europe dreampt of building one is an achievement we would much rather praise than enquire into; without stopping to examine how the thing was done, we have contented ourselves with the fact that it was done. It is time we stopped to ask, "Is it well done?" (From *Makin' Tracks: The Story of the Transcontinental Railroad in the pictures and words of the men who where there,* edited by Lynn Rhodes Mayer and Kenneth E. Vose. New York: Praeger Publishers, Inc., 1975, pp. 147-156)

Some careers were ruined as a result of the railroad's mismanagement, but more fortunes were built. It was decades before all railroad construction in America was completed, and many of the miles of track were financed by taxpayers. The Cental Pacific and Union Pacific also held contracts granting them exclusive rights to freight government goods and troops across the country, at fixed rates—and generous rates they were, too.

It is not surprising that the railroad owners became known as Robber Barons, but other industrialists of the era were just as greedy and manipulative. And as many historians have noted, if the government had not bankrolled the railroads, when would they have been built, and by whom? The railroads opened the vast interior and western portions of the North American continent for development—and the value of that is an incalculable yet impressive return on the taxpayers' investment in the Central Pacific and the Union Pacific Railroads.

Further Reading for Students

Brown, Dee. *Hear that Lonesome Whistle Blow,* New York: Holt, Rinehart and Winston, 1977. For younger readers: *Lonesome Whistle,* New York: Holt, Rinehart & Winston, 1980.

The Railroaders by the editors of Time-Life Books, with text by Keith Wheeler. New York: Time-Life Books, 1973.

Sanfield, Steve. *A Natural Man, the True Story of John Henry,* Boston: David R. Godine, 1986. (for younger readers)

Williams, John Hoyt. *A Great and Shining Road,* New York: Times Books, 1988.

Yep, Laurence. *Dragon's Gate,* New York: Harper Trophy, a division of Harper Collins Publishers. 1993.

About the Editor

Jeanne Munn Bracken wears two professional hats—writer and librarian. Her work at the reference desks of two suburban Boston libraries for the past seventeen years has kindled an abiding fascination with American history. An award-winning columnist for the Littleton (MA) *Independent* for fifteen years, she has written numerous articles and commentaries that have been published in newspapers and magazines from coast to coast. Her books include *Children with Cancer* (Oxford University Press, 1986) and *It All Began With an Apple* (history of the Veryfine Products juice company), 1988 and 1994 editions. She edited *The Shot Heard 'Round the World: The Beginnings of the American Revolution* (1994) for the Perspectives on History Series. Her interest in the westward movement may be in her blood—her great-great-grandfather was one of those who died crossing the Isthmus of Panama in the years before the trans-continental railroad shortened the route. Jeanne lives in Littleton, Massachusetts, with her husband, two daughters, two cats and a rabbit.

The Perspectives on History Series

THE LOWELL MILL GIRLS: Life in the Factory

VOICES FROM THE WEST: Life Along the Trail

COMING TO AMERICA: A New Life in a New Land

FAITH UNFURLED: The Pilgrims' Quest for Freedom

*THE NEW ENGLAND TRANSCENDENTALISTS:
Life of the Mind and of the Spirit*

FORWARD INTO LIGHT: The Struggle for Woman's Suffrage

THE CHEROKEE NATION: Life Before the Tears

PRIDE AND PROMISE: The Harlem Renaissance

EVOLUTION ON TRIAL (The Scopes Trial and Beyond)

THE MANHATTAN PROJECT: A Secret Wartime Mission

*THE SHOT HEARD 'ROUND THE WORLD:
The Beginnings of the American Revolution*

THE PURCHASE OF ALASKA: Folly or Bargain?

*ALL THAT GLITTERS:
The Men and Women of the Gold and Silver Rushes*

WOMEN IN THE CIVIL WAR: Warriors, Patriots, Nurses, and Spies

WESTWARD EXPANSION: Exploration & Settlement

CRY "WITCH": The Salem Witchcraft Trials - 1692

IRON HORSES ACROSS AMERICA: The Transcontinental Railroad

RECONSTRUCTION: Binding the Wounds

*LIFE IN THE AMERICAN COLONIES:
Daily Lifestyles of the Early Settlers*

*COLONIAL TRIANGULAR TRADE:
An Economy Based on Human Misery*

THE GREAT DEPRESSION: A Nation in Distress

THE NEW DEAL: Hope for the Nation

*PRINCIPLES OF DEMOCRACY:
The Constitution and the Bill of Rights*